From the Cross to the Empty Tomb

D1373617

Most Rev. Arthur J. Serratelli
S.T.D., S.S.L., D.D.

CATHOLIC BOOK PUBLISHING CORP.
New Jersey

NIHIL OBSTAT: Rev. T. Kevin Corcoran, MA
Censor Librorum

IMPRIMATUR: ✛ Most Rev. David M. O'Connell, C.M., J.C.D.
Bishop of Trenton

August 21, 2017

The Nihil Obstat and Imprimatur are official declarations that a book or pamphlet is free of doctrinal or moral error. No implication is contained therein that those who have granted the Nihil Obstat and Imprimatur agree with the contents, opinions or statements expressed.

Grateful acknowledgment is made to *The Beacon* for material which appeared previously in its pages.

(T-928)

ISBN 978-1-947070-13-4

© 2017 by Catholic Book Publishing Corp.
77 West End Rd.
Totowa, NJ 07512
Printed in the U.S.A.
www.catholicbookpublishing.com

Contents

Introduction

In ancient times, along Rome's Appian Way, there once stood a sanctuary to the pagan deity the God of Return. Travelers facing long and dangerous journeys would stop here and pray for protection. On their return, they would pause again and give thanks for the happy outcome of their journey. On that very spot, pilgrims still stop, not to visit at a pagan shrine but to pray in the small Church of St. Mary in Palmis, commonly called "the Church of the *Quo Vadis.*"

Quo Vadis is Latin for "where are you going." According to tradition, when persecution broke out against the Christians in Rome under Nero, Peter decided to leave the city. He was fleeing for his life. Then, on this spot, he met Jesus headed in the opposite direction, back into the city. Peter asked Him, *"Domine, quo vadis" ("Lord, where are you going?").* And Jesus answered: *"I am going to Rome to be crucified again."* Peter immediately understood. He followed Jesus back to Rome where he was crucified. Strengthened by the Lord, the fearful fugitive became the courageous apostle who willingly gave his life in witness to Jesus.

The life of every Christian is a continual sharing in the Cross. Not just in the first century of ancient Rome, but, in every age, there is the temptation to run, like Peter, from the hostility and persecution that we face in living as a true follower of Jesus. The world does not value all that Jesus taught. It tries to get us not to live as Jesus teaches. So often it tempts us to say not *"thy will be done,"* but *"my will be done."* Each day, we need to die to self so as to follow Jesus. For this reason, Tertullian called Christians *crucis religiosi*, i.e., *"devotees of the Cross"* (*Apology*, xvi).

Jesus' death on the Cross had been no common death. Our guilt condemned the innocent One. Our shameless deeds fashioned the ignominy of the Cross. Our sinful pleasure pierced Him through with unutterable pain. Knowing what was before Him, Jesus once said, *"No one takes my life from me, but I lay it down on my own"* (Jn 10:18). Jesus had gone to the Cross, because this was God's will to accomplish our redemption. As Pope St. John Paul II wrote in his first encyclical, *Redemptor Hominis*, *"The God of creation is revealed as the God of redemption, as the God who is 'faithful to himself,' and faithful to his love for man and the world, which he revealed on the day of creation"* (n. 9). God is love and remains true to His will to save us even in the face of our human sinfulness.

As Christians, we make our life-journey in union with Christ Crucified. The *via crucis* is the school of Christian life. As Peter once asked Jesus, the world questions each of us today, *"Quo Vadis?"* "Where are you going?" It will help each of us respond to this question by accompanying Jesus on the Way to the Cross. I offer the following brief meditations on individuals who were with Jesus in the last hours of His own life on earth.

Peter

1

The Gift of Forgiveness

In Shakespeare's *Romeo and Juliet*, a family feud prevents Juliet from marrying Romeo. Juliet laments that it is simply Romeo's name that keeps him from her. She complains, "What's in a name? That which we call a rose / By any other name would smell as sweet." Yet, names do have meaning. God changes Abram's name to Abraham—giving him the special mission of being the father of the chosen people (see Gen 17:5). God changes Jacob's name to Israel ("the one who prevails with God"). He is promising that the chosen people who issue from the loins of this patriarch would bear the blessing of salvation through much suffering (see Gen 35:10-12). In the Old Testament, names can bear the burden of a person's role in salvation history.

So, too, in the New Testament. A new name comes to mean a new mission. Jesus calls Simon "Cephas" or "Rock" (see Mt 16:18). This Aramaic word is translated in Greek as *Petros* and, in English, as Peter. Jesus uses this name to indicate the new role Peter will have as the leader of the other disciples. This is the only time Jesus changes the name of one of His disciples. A unique moment. A singular mission for Peter.

Over the course of His public ministry, Jesus makes clear to Peter his place as leader. He chooses Peter's lakeside house in Capernaum to be the headquarters of his Galilean ministry. When the question arises about Jesus and taxes, Jesus responds by paying the temple tax for Himself and Peter (see Mt 17:24-27). At the Last Supper, Jesus singles out Peter as the one who will strengthen the other disciples in faith (see Lk 22:32).

Already in the life of Jesus, Peter takes on a special role. He speaks out in the name of the others. He asks Jesus to explain what He means when He tells a parable (see Mt 15:15). He questions what Jesus is teaching when He lays down a rule for community living (see Mt 18:21) and when He makes the promise of a reward (see Mt 19:27).

The gospels pay special attention both to the highs and lows of Peter's special ministry. The day after the multiplication of the loaves and fish, Jesus explains the miracle in the synagogue of Capernaum. He gives the first promise of the Eucharist. As a result, many people stop following Jesus. His words about giving His flesh as the bread of life are just too much. Speaking for the other apostles, Peter voices the loyalty of every true believer. *"Lord, to whom shall we go? You have the words of eternal life; and we have believed, and have come to know, that you are the Holy One of God"* (Jn 6:66-69).

At Caesarea Philippi, Peter is the very first to voice the faith of the Church that Jesus is the Christ, the long-awaited Messiah (see Mt 16:16-17). At the Last Supper, Peter professes total loyalty to Jesus, even to death (see Mk 14:31). And, during the arrest of Jesus in Gethsemane, Peter wields his sword like a freedom fighter ready to join Jesus in overthrowing Rome (see Jn 18:10)—confident, bold, impetuous Peter.

At the Last Supper, Jesus predicts Peter's fall. He says, *"Simon, Simon, Satan has desired to sift you [plural] like wheat. But I have prayed that your own faith may not fail. And once you [singular] have turned back, you [singular] must strengthen your brothers"* (Lk 22:31-32). Jesus tells all of the disciples of Satan's desire to make them fall. But, then, Jesus singles out Peter. He calls him affectionately, "Simon, Simon."

Jesus uses the name Peter had before Jesus changed it. Jesus is reminding Peter of his former life, of his human weakness apart from walking in the company of Jesus.

Jesus warns Peter of his lapse in discipleship. He also offers him the assistance of His prayer. Peter is the leader of the apostles. The danger he faces is greater than the rest. When a leader fails or falters, the entire community suffers. Therefore, Jesus makes special intercession for the disciple whose fall causes the greatest harm to others.

So, too, today. Those called to the service of leadership have a special place in the intercessory prayer of Christ. What a great comfort! There is no leader without sin. No one is sinless. Not even those who are ready to uncover the alleged sins of others.

The prediction of Peter's failure in discipleship serves as a warning that the call to grace requires our cooperation. God's favor does not negate our human freedom. Our vocation as Christians is something we have to work out *"in fear and trembling"* (Phil 2:12). God gifts us with His love. But, love cannot be constrained. In the circumstances of our life, we need to respond. And, in dark moments, we need to turn to the light.

Within a very few hours of the Last Supper, Jesus' prediction comes true. The Rock is pulverized. Peter denies Jesus. Peter is the most assertive disciple in all the gospels. Even in failure, he takes the lead. In the courtyard of the high priest, three times Peter denies Jesus. All the gospels tell us that a cock crows as Peter is denying Jesus. It is in the early hours of the morning, somewhere between 3 and 5 a.m. And Peter remembers Jesus' words: *"Before the cock crows twice, you will deny me three times"* (Mk 14:72).

Luke alone gives us the following detail. *"At that instant, while he was still speaking, the cock crowed, and the Lord turned and looked straight at Peter, and Peter remembered the Lord's words…"* (Lk 22:60-62). Even as nature accuses the sinner, the Lord of all creation looks at Peter with love.

Jesus looked at Peter. Peter could deny Jesus at a distance. But when he is close enough for Jesus to look at him, he can no longer stand apart. How much better our lives would be if we were to always live in the presence of the Lord. The sinner is never out of the Lord's sight. The Lord sees us every moment of our lives. We go about our work. We enjoy the good things of this world. Sometimes we try to escape notice as one of His disciples. Yet the Lord sees. And His look is beyond that of the judge pronouncing the sentence of guilty. As long as we are on this earth, His look is that of the compassionate Savior who longs to lift us up.

Judas had betrayed Jesus. Then he went out and hanged himself. Peter denied Jesus. Then he went out and wept bitterly. Judas had remorse; Peter, repentance. Peter realized that he had betrayed love. He had not let Jesus make him the man that Jesus wanted him to be. Judas turned in on himself and despaired. Peter turned to the Lord and repented. For one, death. For the other, a whole new life.

Peter is the first disciple mentioned in the Gospel of Mark. He is also the last named. He shows both the beginning and the end of our following of Jesus. We move from accepting Jesus' call, through times of faith and failure, to the moment when we entrust all that we are to His grace. Discipleship is *"not a triumphal march but a journey marked daily by suffering and love, trials and faithfulness"* (Pope Benedict XVI, Wednesday Audience, May 24, 2006).

The story of Peter's denial is gospel. His fall is a lesson in both sin and grace. It is a story we should never forget. Through the Church that Jesus founded on Peter, God continues to offer forgiveness to sinners. Through her faithful preaching of the gospel and her celebration of the sacraments, the Church brings sinners face to face with the Savior whose look of love can melt sin away and move the hardest heart to tears.

"Even my trusted friend on whom I relied, who shared my table, lifts his heel against me" (Ps 41:9).

Judas
2
The *Mystery of Iniquity*

Benedict Arnold, Quisling, Ethel and Julius Rosenberg—history never forgets the names of those who have turned traitor. And, at the head of the list stands the name Judas. In every place he is mentioned in the gospels, the evangelists never fail to mention that he was the one who betrayed Jesus. No one can be neutral to a traitor.

If a cause is betrayed, there is great anger. If a person well-loved and doing good is betrayed, there is a sickening feeling of loathing for the one who hands another over. Certainly this seems to be the feeling among the early Christians.

So appalled were Matthew, Mark, and Luke that they could not bear to speak about Judas. They kept a marked silence except when it comes to tell of his sin. From these evangelists, we receive no information from the time of Judas' call when he begins to walk with Jesus until he walks away and betrays him at the end of his life.

Christians have tried to make sense of how one individual, chosen by Jesus, loved as a trusted friend, could have then placed Jesus in the hands of the very enemies who were already plotting to destroy the most innocent man the world has ever known. Writing sometime after the Christian community has meditated on the sin of Judas, the fourth evangelist fills in some of the details. But, these only darken the portrait of the man who sold his Master for a few pieces of silver.

In the story of the Passion, Matthew shows a particular interest in the question of responsibility. Who is responsible for the death of Jesus? Mark, the first gospel writer, answers this question with the story of Judas' going to the priests to arrange the handing over of Jesus. Matthew fills in the details (see Mt 27:3-10).

According to Matthew, Judas goes back to the priests after the arrest of Jesus. He flings the thirty pieces of silver across the temple floor. Each coin crashes against the cold marble shouting out his crime. He betrayed the Master for the price of a slave (see Ex 21:32). The chief priests refuse to accept the money. It is contaminated. So in an attempt to free themselves of blood money, the money is used to buy Akeldama (the Field of Blood) to bury the dead. For

Matthew, it is not just Judas who is guilty for the blood of an innocent man. It is the chief priests and all who, by their sins, cry out for his death (see Mt 27:25).

Matthew is writing his gospel somewhere after 70 A.D. The temple has already been destroyed. People are questioning: "What did we do to deserve this?" No doubt some members of his community look to the death of Jesus for quick answers to a very tangled question. The Church clearly teaches Jesus' betrayal is the sin of each one of us. It is not the crime or treachery of one individual, or one group of people, let alone an entire race. Christ died for *all* sinners.

The Apocryphal Arabic *Gospel of the Infancy* paints the darkest picture of all. This sixth century gospel portrays Judas as possessed by Satan even in his childhood. In this way, he is seen as totally outside the influence of Jesus. But such an explanation is too facile. Jesus did choose Judas. He knew he would betray Him. These facts are clear from the inspired gospels. What we face in the figure of Judas is *"the mystery of iniquity"* (2 Thes 2:7).

At the Last Supper, Jesus makes the sad announcement: *"One of you is about to betray me."* Fear strikes dread in the hearts of the apostles. In the midst of the festive meal among close friends, a somber prophecy of disloyalty is made, echoing what the psalmist said, *"Even my trusted friend on whom I relied, who shared my table, lifts his heel against me"* (Ps 41:9).

All of the apostles respond in horror, *"Is it I, Lord?"* In the Greek, the question is so framed that the negative response is anticipated. None of them can think of himself as turning against his friend and Master. And yet, they are unsure of themselves. And even more interesting, Judas does not ask the same question as the other apostles.

Every individual is capable of sin. Some are inclined to sins of weakness. And then there are the self-righteous who set themselves over others in judgment and condemnation. Their sin is deeper. It is pride—the sin of Lucifer. At the root of all sin is the self that exalts itself over and against God who wills what is good for us and who Himself is love and mercy without limit. No individual with a human heart is so sure of himself that he is safe in pointing the finger at another. All of us need to ask, "Is it I, Lord?"

The Christian has the courage to ask, "Is it I, Lord?" For the Christian can face the answer: "Yes, I have betrayed my Master." The Christian knows that the heart of God is love. The Christian knows that, "... *the greatest sin on man's part is matched, in the heart of the Redeemer, by the oblation of supreme love that conquers the evil of all the sins of man. On the basis of this certainty ... [we do] not hesitate to repeat every year, at the Easter Vigil, 'O happy fault!'"* (Pope St. John Paul II, *Dominum et vivificantem*, 31).

"So in the end Pilate handed him over to them to be crucified" (Jn 19:16).

Pilate

3

The Challenge of Conscience

Near Lucerne, Switzerland rises 7,000 foot high Mt. Pilatus. Here Pontius Pilate, legend says, traveled when removed from office in 37 A.D. Here he died. A long way from Jerusalem where history remembers the most important public decision he ever made. Even farther has Pilate traveled in the imagination of Christians. The greater the distance from the pages of Scripture, the more virtuous Pilate becomes.

In the East, Tertullian gives him a Christian heart (*Apologeticum* 21.18.24). Augustine sees him as a prophet (*Sermo* 201). And seventh century Copts make him a saint. They even baptize their children with his name. In the West, Pilate's memory moves in the opposite direction. In medieval Passion plays, he is a sinister individual with little affinity with the message of Jesus. Tradition has done him no injustice. For in the story of the Passion of Jesus, Pilate is both noble and ignoble, both open and closed to the truth.

In 26 A.D. Pilate arrived in Caesarea Marittima to govern Judea as the Roman prefect. He immediately sent his troops to Jerusalem to assert his authority. The soldiers carried standards bearing pagan images offensive to the Jews. So he sent them at night. Pilate was knowledgeable, but not wise; political, but not prudent. For six days the Jews protested the pagan images in the holy city. When threatened with death, they protested even louder. Pilate gave in to the pressure. Rome had given the Jews autonomy of religion, and Pilate dare not offend Rome.

On another occasion, Pilate angered the Jews and did not give in. When building an aqueduct into Jerusalem, he took money from the temple treasury. Thousands protested. Pilate responded with force and many perished. Rome expected order in the province. Pilate carefully guarded his political position. He did it well. He had one of the longest tenures of any prefect in Judea. For ten years, he ruled. From the time of John the Baptist until the birth of the Church, he was Rome to both the Jews and Christians of Judea.

It is to Pilate that Jesus is brought on political charges. Jesus is a threat to the emperor. He is claiming to be "King of the Jews." Throughout His ministry, Jesus' teaching brought Him into conflict with the members of His own faith community. He faced religious opposition. Now Jesus' own hurl Him before Pilate and accuse Him of political opposition to Rome. So strong is their animosity that they want nothing less than the sentence of death.

The secular and the religious, the human and the divine stand face to face as Jesus comes before Pilate. No government, no secular authority, no political party has a monopoly on the truth. The state needs to be open to an understanding about life that comes from religion. A government that ignores or rejects such truth inflicts injustice on its people. Truth is truth. And only truth sets us free (see Jn 8:32). Rejecting Jesus, who is Truth itself, Pilate becomes the prisoner.

All four evangelists tend not to put all the blame for the death of Jesus on Pilate. Mark paints Pilate as a poor excuse for Roman justice. In the three other gospels, his portrait is not so unflattering. In fact, John emphasizes his desire to do what is right. During the trial of Jesus, the crowd gathers outside the praetorium. Jesus is held within. On the outside, frenzied anger. People shout. Their hatred for Jesus pressuring Pilate to pervert justice and condemn Him. On the inside, calm and the semblance of justice. Pilate questions and examines Jesus. Four times Pilate goes back and forth, in and out, between the noise of the street and the quiet of the court. Two opposing judgments; one choice. It is the struggle of conscience.

On the outside, the verdict of guilt is demanded. On the inside, the verdict of innocence is proven. In fact, three different times, Pilate acknowledges the innocence of Jesus (see Jn 18:38; 19:4; 19:6). Three times, he tries to escape making a final choice between the crowd and Jesus.

First, he makes the crowd choose between Barabbas and Jesus. Barabbas is a known murderer. Pilate is appealing to their sense of justice. They choose to set Barabbas free. Their consciences are dead.

Next, he appeals to their sense of compassion. He has Jesus brutally scourged. He himself watches. He does not want the prisoner to die. He brings Jesus, flogged and scourged, purpled in his own blood and crowned with thorns, saying, *"Behold the man"* (Jn 19:5). Sheer pity for the suffering is powerful. But they cry out, *"Crucify him, crucify him"* (Jn 19:6). Their hearts are hardened. Pilate is not so callous. *"From that moment, Pilate was anxious to set him free"* (Jn 19:12).

He makes one final and desperate attempt to free Jesus. The Jews were forcing him to do what he would not. He forces them to do what they should not. They keep shouting at him, *"If you set him free, you are no friend of Caesar…"* (Jn 19:12). Pilate fears the threat. He can remain ruler only as long as he is loyal to Rome. With contempt in his voice, he provokes the crowd to blasphemy. *"'Do you want me to crucify your king?' Pilate asked them"* (Jn 19:15a).

God is Israel's king in heaven; the Messiah, His king on earth. *"The chief priests answered, 'We have no king except Caesar'"* (Jn 19:15b). They deny their faith along with their national hope for freedom. *"So in the end Pilate handed him over to them to be crucified"* (Jn 19:16). Pilate has washed his hands of the matter (see Mt 27:23-25). But, the stain of guilt cannot be erased.

In the story of the Passion, Pilate is not simply the state against religion. He is not Rome against Jerusalem. Rather Pilate is each of us who must choose for or against Christ and His gospel. Pilate confronts us with the reality of conscience.

As followers of Jesus, we need to have a well-formed conscience. We need to look beyond our feelings and beyond our preferences. Since goodness finds its source within God, the process of forming our conscience places us in an intimate, personal dialogue with God Himself (see Pope St. John Paul II, *Veritatis Splendor*, 60). Our conscience is a gift meant to lift us up to heaven itself.

As humans, we can be mistaken. Sometimes ignorance clouds our discernment; sometimes, sin. But, a well-formed conscience will not contradict the truth Jesus teaches us through His Church. A properly formed conscience will always lead us to make those moral choices that accept Jesus as *"the Way, the Truth, and the Life"* (Jn 14:6).

Barabbas

4

True Freedom

No character of the Passion leaves us with a lingering question more than Barabbas. His story is broken off before it concludes. Barabbas was a "bandit" (see Jn 18:40) and much more than a petty thief.

Both Mark and Luke brand Barabbas as a murderer (see Mk 15:11; Lk 23:19). He is a troublemaker who incited people to riot. This was not difficult at a time when Zealots were ready with sword in hand to overthrow the Roman oppressors. In the eyes of the people, the Zealots were patriots. For the government, they were terrorists. Zealots were everywhere, even among Jesus' chosen friends. In listing the twelve apostles, Luke labels Simon "the Zealot." And the surname of Judas Iscariot could well mean *"sicarius,"* or "dagger man."

Not one of the gospels gives us the names of either of the two criminals crucified to the right and left of Jesus. But, every one of them remembers the name of Barabbas. They could not forget him. He was notorious. This prisoner was a well-known ringleader who caused harm even to his own people. He is guilty of the very crime falsely leveled against Jesus: subverting the authority of Caesar.

Barabbas' name is very interesting. Ancient manuscripts of the gospel text give us his full name as Jesus Barabbas. In the first century, Jesus or Joshua was not an uncommon name. That is why it was common to add a patronymic to it. Jesus is called *"Jesus, Bar Joseph, from Nazareth"* (Jn 1:45; see 6:42). Barabbas would therefore be a surname.

The patronymic "Barabbas" is a contraction of two words, "Bar" or "son" and "Abba." "Abba" could either be a man's first name or the Aramaic word for "father" or "daddy." In copying the gospel texts, ancient scribes took it upon themselves to copy only this man's surname. Like the famous theologian Origen, they could not bear a wicked person bearing the same first name as the Savior.

All the gospels tell us that Pilate tried to free Jesus by offering the crowds the choice between Barabbas and Jesus. Pilate knows that Jesus has been handed over to him because the leaders of the people were envious. Jesus had too much influence over the people. Jealousy also played a part in handing the apostles Peter and Paul over for their martyrdom. *"Through envy and jealousy, the greatest and most righteous pillars [of the Church] have been persecuted and put to death"* (1 Clement 5:12). Envy also divided the community of Corinth. Envy causes great harm.

It was the Passover custom to release a prisoner in celebration of the Jews' great feast of liberation. Pilate takes the occasion to rid himself of condemning an innocent man to death. He places the choice before the rabble: Jesus or Barabbas.

Crowds are notoriously fickle. Herod the Great rebuilt the temple in Jerusalem. Insensitive to the religious fervor of the Jews, he placed a golden eagle on the gate. This symbol of Roman power outraged the Jews. Some young men were encouraged by their rabbis to tear it down. The crowds joined in and promised support. When the Romans caught forty of these young men tearing the eagle down, the people feared for themselves and withdrew support. The young men were summarily executed (see Josephus, *The Jewish Wars*, 1.33.3). Selfish interests too easily cast principle to the wind!

Some in the crowd that gather around Pilate had welcomed Jesus into Jerusalem just six days before. Their throats are still hoarse from shouting their "Hosannas." Now they begin to shout for Jesus' death.

Pressure from a small, well-organized group that had turned on Jesus incited them to demand the death penalty (see Mk 15:11). Pressure groups still sway politicians and legislators to make decisions against justice and the common good. It takes a strong individual to stand apart from the crowd and hold firm to principle.

There were many struggles within Jerusalem against the Romans. Rebels were routinely crucified as an example for others. Eventually the constant unrest precipitated Jewish aristocracy's loss of control both of the city and their temple. When some of the Jewish leaders incite the crowd to call for the release of Barabbas, they are actually contributing to the loss of their own authority. Doing evil to others ultimately harms us more than the ones we seek to harm.

The choice Pilate offers the crowd is dramatic: two men. The one is called the Christ.

He is innocent and sinless. He is the true Son of the Father. The other is called Barabbas. He is guilty and sinful. Both men have the same first name, Jesus.

The crowd is swayed. Luke tells us, *"As one man, they howled, 'Away with this man! Give us Barabbas!'"* (Lk 23:18). In the synagogue of Capernaum, the man possessed by a demon "howled" after Jesus (see Lk 4:33). The Gerasene demoniac also "howled" at the top of his voice (see Lk 8:28). The crowd now "howls." Their evil is more than human. This is the hour of Satan. In choosing Barabbas, they side with Satan. Justice is perverted; innocence condemned. Public opinion is not always right, but it is always strong. It can do much violence to the innocent.

Pilate is weak. Though he was willing to save Jesus, he is unwilling to destroy his career by having the people turn against him. He yields to the crowd's persistent cries. They shout for the one who promises political freedom by the sword. They reject the One who brings true freedom through love. The choice of Barabbas unmasks the populace's ideal. They want a Messiah to take up arms against Rome. They admire the rebel, not the peacemaker. We can always be judged by the heroes we admire.

Jesus is taken to be crucified; Barabbas goes free. Jesus' death is more than just one man dying instead of another. It is the Just One dying *for all others*. His death atones for the sins of the world.

Here ends the story of the murderer let loose on society. Barabbas knows that Jesus is dying in his place. But we have no way of knowing what effect this has on him. Is he moved to repentance? Does he return to his old ways? Does he use the new freedom to do good? The gospels leave unsaid what choice Barabbas makes with his new gift of freedom. Wisely so. Barabbas is each of us for whom Jesus died. We need to answer that question for ourselves!

5 Simon of Cyrene
Discipleship

Cicero, the great forensic orator and philosopher of the first century before Christ, called the Cross "a most cruel and disgusting penalty" (*In Verrem* 2.5.64.66). The Roman playwright Seneca, living at the time of Christ, said, *"the very name 'cross' should not only be far from the body of a Roman citizen, but also from his thoughts, his eyes and his ear"* (*Epistle* 101.14).

Crucifixion had been practiced long before the Romans began to use it as a punishment for the lower class members of society. Slaves, soldiers, and criminals were crucified. Roman citizens were spared. In the East, the Greeks would impale a criminal already executed and dead on a cross as a social deterrent. The Romans perfected the cruelty. They crucified their victims alive—always on a crowded street. The death was slow; the agony, long. And many people could watch. It was a brutal recompense for offenses against the state.

As the soldiers lead Jesus to a little hill outside a gate leading into Jerusalem, they begin to worry. The spectators might miss their show. The scourging had been too fierce. The pieces of bone fastened to the leather straps that had lashed again and again against the body of Jesus had ripped open His flesh. The blood was bathing the pavement. Some criminals never made it to the cross. The soldiers fear Jesus will die before Pilate's order for crucifixion is carried out.

The gruesome parade passes through the city walls. The onlookers press close to see the victim. Some simply scorn His suffering. Others feel pity for His undeserved plight. The anxious soldiers catch sight of a man coming in from the countryside. Mark identifies this man as *"a passer-by, Simon of Cyrene, father of Alexander and Rufus"* (Mk 15:21). Simon is stumbling into one of the most unforgettable parts in the drama of redemption. Luke tells us they grab hold of him. The Greek word *epilambanesthai* conjures up the image of the soldiers' hands reaching out and seizing Simon (see Lk 23:26). They press him into service. In fact, the very word Mark and Matthew use, the Greek word *aggareuein*, indicates someone being forced into government service (see Mk 15:21; Mt 27:32).

However, Simon is being pressed into the service of an authority higher than Rome. The soldiers place the crossbeam on him. The upright beam was already in place at the site of execution, awaiting its victim. Simon is compelled to carry Jesus' burden of the crossbeam. In the Sermon on the Mount, Jesus laid down the law of the kingdom of God. He had said, *"if someone forces you to carry his pack one mile, carry it two miles"* (Mt 5:41). Thus the unwelcome necessity becomes a cheerful grace. In accepting the Cross of Christ on his shoulders, Simon fulfills that law.

Simon drags the crossbeam. Luke points out that he carries it behind Jesus (see Lk 23:26). Jesus goes first; Simon physically walks in His footsteps. Jesus leads; Simon follows. It is the way of discipleship. Simon is literally beginning his walk with Jesus.

Jesus stops His own funeral procession and consoles the weeping woman of Jerusalem. Simon listens. Even in His suffering, Jesus thinks more of others' fate than His own. His vision is not blurred by the blood falling from His brow. He sees to the ultimate consequences of sin and warns the woman to repent. This is more than human. Good example, even at great cost to oneself and in the most painful of circumstances, is not without effect. Simon is moved. From the unwilling passer-by, he becomes the generous cooperator with Jesus in His redemptive death.

Simon comes from Cyrene, a capital city in North Africa. There were Jews in that city (see Acts 6:9; 11:20; 13:1). Simon's name could be either Jewish or Greek. There is no way of knowing whether he is a Jew or Gentile. And this is not without meaning. As Paul teaches, *"There is no difference between Jew and Greek, between slaves and freemen, between men and women, all of you are one in union with Christ Jesus"* (Gal 3.28). All people are called to salvation in Christ. "... *Jesus Christ has a significance and a value for the human race and its history, which are unique and singular, proper to him alone, exclusive, universal, and absolute. Jesus is, in fact, the Word of God made man for the salvation of all"* (*Dominus Jesus*, 15). All of us are called to carry the cross of Christ.

Tradition astutely identifies Simon as a Christian. Mark makes a point of reminding us that Simon was the father of Alexander and Rufus. This little detail informs us that these two individuals were well known to the community for which the evangelist writes his gospel. Following in the footsteps of Jesus along the Via Dolorosa, Simon led the way for his family. The faith of a parent spills over into the home and provides the environment for the children to become strong Christians. Good example is the best teacher.

The soldiers conscripted Simon to be part of Jesus' death march. They made sure they had a victim to offer up to the demanding rabble. But their actions did much more. They etched into the memory of Christian tradition an unforgettable image of true discipleship. The Christians who first read Mark's gospel were facing persecution and death in Rome. To those first century Christians and to Christians of every age and place who face opposition and persecution and at times even death, Simon remains a living monument of Jesus' words, *"If anyone wants to come after me, let him deny himself and take up his cross every day and follow me"* (Lk 9:23). The cross is not a coincidence in the Christian life. It is the very plan of salvation.

"Daughters of Jerusalem, do not weep for me; weep instead for yourselves and for your children" (Lk 23:28).

6 Daughters of Jerusalem
Repentance

The Via Sacra was the main street of
ancient Rome. It passed through some
of the most important pagan temples in the
Forum. Along this road, Rome would stage
the celebrations of her military strength.
Today, at what was once the highest point
of this road stands the Arch of Titus. This
monument commemorates the triumphal
procession of Titus into Rome after his
destruction of Jerusalem in 70 A.D.

Ancient Rome lavishly celebrated her
great victories. After successful military
campaigns, the conquering hero would
enter the city of Rome in triumph. A great
procession escorted him from the outskirts
of the city along the Via Sacra to the Forum.
Seasoned soldiers with carts loaded with
spoils of war proudly marched amid the
cheers of the crowd. Captives and slaves
walked humiliated before the returning
general in his chariot drawn by white hors-
es. Such a sight thrilled the Romans with
its parade of prowess and pride. Roman
arches, reliefs, and coins kept the memory

of such displays of power alive in the minds of the people.

How different the triumphal entry of Jesus into Jerusalem at the beginning of His last week on earth! Jesus enters the city of Jerusalem amid the joyful shouts of the crowd. He is riding not on a horse used for war, but on a donkey. He comes not as the military warrior whom many were expecting, but as the Messiah who comes in peace. Those accompanying Him raise their voices in grateful Hosannas. They praise God for all the miracles that Jesus has done. But their loud acclaim cannot silence the sorrow in the heart of Jesus. He knows what lies ahead. The road is set in the direction of Calvary.

As the Palm Sunday procession makes its way to the crest of the Mount of Olives, Jesus sees the city of Jerusalem spread out before Him. What a view! The Temple rising high above the horizon; its white marble and gold dazzling in the light of the setting sun! The words of the Psalmist make Jesus pause and think: *"The holy mountain, fairest of heights, the joy of all the earth, Mount Zion, the heights of Zaphon, the city of the great king"* (Ps 48:3-4). This is the season of Passover. It is a time of joy and celebration.

This is freedom's feast. But Jesus stretches His eyes beyond the city crowded with Passover pilgrims and sees the fate that awaits those who do not turn from sin.

"As Jesus drew near, he saw the city and wept over it, saying, 'If this day you only knew what makes for peace—but now it is hidden from your eyes. For the days are coming upon you when your enemies will raise a palisade against you; they will encircle you and hem you in on all sides. They will smash you to the ground and your children within you, and they will not leave one stone upon another within you because you did not recognize the time of your visitation'" (Lk 19:42-44).

Right before the destruction of Jerusalem by the Babylonians in the sixth century B.C., the prophet Jeremiah had pleaded with the people to return to God in order to avert the impending doom. But, when they did not, he lamented their hard-heartedness, saying, *"My eyes will run with tears for the Lord's flock"* (Jer 13:17). Like Jeremiah, Jesus weeps over the destruction of Jerusalem and the fate of His people in His own day. But Jesus is more than a prophet. He is the Son of God. He sees more than just one city.

For Jesus, Jerusalem symbolizes the world. God gives beyond measure to all His people. He calls out again and again for us to accept His will. He longs for the gift of our hearts. He desires to fill them with peace. Yet, age after age, so many of us turn a deaf ear to His appeal. For Jesus, Jerusalem is all of us, unbelieving and indifferent to God's providence.

On the way to the Cross, Jesus again speaks of the destruction of the Holy City. He tells the women of Jerusalem to mourn not for Him, but for themselves and the coming destruction of their city. He says, *"Daughters of Jerusalem, do not weep for me; weep instead for yourselves and for your children, for indeed, the days are coming when people will say, 'Blessed are the barren, the wombs that never bore and the breasts that never nursed.' At that time people will say to the mountains, 'Fall upon us!' and to the hills, 'Cover us!' For if these things are done when the wood is green, what will happen when it is dry?"* (Lk 23:28-31). When Titus soon comes to torch the city and destroy the Temple and Jerusalem, Jesus' words will be fulfilled.

The same message that Jesus spoke to the women of Jerusalem, He publicly had spoken to all. When teaching in the Temple on the Tuesday of the last week of His life, Jesus spoke vividly in apocalyptic terms about the coming destruction. He said, *"When you see Jerusalem surrounded by armies, know that her desolation is at hand . . . for these days are the time of punishment. . . .Woe to pregnant women and nursing mothers in those days, for a terrible calamity will come upon the earth, and a wrathful judgment upon this people. They will fall by the edge of the sword and be taken as captives to all the Gentiles, and Jerusalem will be trampled underfoot by the Gentiles. . . ."* (Lk 21:20-24; see also Mt 24:15-21; Mk 13:14-19).

In repeating this message to the women of Jerusalem before He is crucified, Jesus quotes a proverb. He says, *"If these things are done when the wood is green, what will happen when it is dry?"* (Lk 23:31). What do these enigmatic words of Jesus mean?

In the proverb, the green wood is placed in opposition to the dry wood. The green wood represents a time when things are flourishing and there is freedom to grow. The dry wood represents a time when life becomes barren and arid, when life is oppressive and difficult. In the proverb, the passive voice is used. This is a polite way to avoid naming the intended subjects. But, the subjects can easily be supplied. In the first part of the proverb, the subject is the Jewish people; in the second part, it is the Romans.

With this proverb, Jesus is telling His own people that, if they treat Him as they do with such cruelty in His Passion and Death when they are not being forced to do so by the Romans, how much more harshly will the Romans treat them when they deal with their rebellion. Jesus is delicately predicting the inevitable consequence of turning from the truth that God gives us. His warning is not limited to the people of His day.

Jesus sees us hastening toward self-destruction. He went to the Cross for our salvation, but not without the sorrow of knowing how difficult it is to reach our sinful hearts. From deep within His soul, there arose a sorrow that could not contain itself. And so Jesus wept! What a sight! The Son of God weeping not for the suffering that He would soon endure in His Passion and Death, but weeping for us! Should we not be moved? Should we not take to heart His words to the women of Jerusalem? Should we not weep tears of repentance for the sins we commit?

Jesus' final words before He mounts the Cross inject a dose of reality into our thinking about God. Jesus had warned the crowds and His followers again and again that if they did not repent, there would be wailing and gnashing of teeth (see Mt 8:11-12; Mt 22:12-13; Mt 24:50-51; Mt 25:29-30; Lk 13:27-28). God is all holy and He is all just. There can be no evil in His sight. We are created in freedom. God leaves us free to respond to His love. When life is going well, when we spend our time earning a good living, caring for our family, enjoying the pleasures of this world, we can become lulled into thinking that our sins do not matter. But evil choices have consequences and we cannot escape them.

Our sins of selfishness, anger, envy, lust, pride, and avarice cause suffering to others and to ourselves. God takes no pleasure in this suffering. He does not inflict punishment on us with the vengeance of an unrequited lover. Rather, He himself sorrows over the harm that we do to ourselves and others. He feels our pain so much that He sends His only-begotten Son to be our Savior. *"God did not spare his own Son but handed him over for all of us"* (Rm 8:31).

Jesus' triumphant entry into Jerusalem takes Him to the Cross, but does not end there. Through His suffering and death, the Crucified Christ enters the glory of heaven where He prepares a place for us. He makes it possible for us to avoid the punishment that our sins merit in the life to come. He turns our tears of repentance into the triumph of grace over sin. For, through the mystery of His Passion, Death, and Resurrection, Christ takes away our sins and imparts to us a share in God's own life in this world and, in the next, a share in His glory.

The Crowd
Divine Grace

In the first century, Jerusalem was one of the largest cities between Alexandria in Egypt and Damascus in Syria. Herod the Great had ushered in the city's renaissance with his vast building projects. He reorganized the city's serpentine streets into a paved grid. He built himself a palace with luxury bedrooms for one hundred guests. In the midst of the crowded city, his palace was a walled resort. A network of underground cisterns collected rainwater and made its gardens green and refreshing (see Flavius Josephus, *The Wars of the Jews,* Book 5, 4).

Herod also constructed an amphitheater and a hippodrome for the enjoyment of the people. And, as his crowning achievement, he reconstructed the Temple, making it a wonder of the ancient world. Jerusalem was truly a cosmopolitan city, prosperous and inviting.

Each year when Passover came, pilgrims would flood the city, swelling its population from eighty thousand to two hundred and fifty thousand. For the Jews, Passover was the most important feast. It commemorated their deliverance from Egyptian bondage. According to all four gospels, Jesus was crucified in Jerusalem during the Passover celebrations when the city was throbbing with activity. It is no surprise, then, that Luke tells us that *"a large crowd of people followed Jesus, including many women who mourned and lamented him"* (Lk 23:27).

The spectacle of a man being led out of the city to be crucified could not go unnoticed. In fact, the Roman authorities would make every effort to have the condemned man walk a path that would attract the greatest attention. They wanted his cruel fate to be seen by as many people as possible. In this way, it could serve as a warning to anyone who would even think of opposing Rome.

Although Jesus had only spent a short time of His public ministry in Jerusalem (see Mt 21:10-11), He, nonetheless, was well known. Many had heard of His miracles. Only recently, He had healed a beggar at the Pool of Bethseda in the North of Jerusalem (see Jn 5) and the blind man at the Pool of Siloam in the South of Jerusalem (see Jn 9). So well known was Jesus that His enemies feared His arrest would cause a great disturbance (see Mk 14:2).

When the two disciples on the road to Emmaus spoke with Jesus, unaware of His identity, they were astonished at His apparent ignorance of the events surrounding the crucifixion. One of them, Cleopas, asks, *"Are you the only visitor to Jerusalem who is not aware of all the things that have taken place there in these days?...The things that happened to Jesus the Nazarene, who was a prophet mighty in word and deed before God and all the people, how our chief priests and rulers handed him over to a sentence of death and crucified him"* (Lk 24:18-20). Christ's crucifixion was a most public event.

Luke is the only evangelist to report the presence of a large crowd that follows Jesus. Perhaps, Luke is thinking of those individuals who were present in Pilate's praetorium and had shouted for His crucifixion. When Pilate had offered to release Jesus in honor of the Passover, they had demanded, instead, the release of Barabbas, a known murderer. The crowd had been manipulated by Jesus' enemies.

Crowds are easily manipulated. The anonymity of the crowd masks personal responsibility. People in crowds think differently than when they are on their own. We need always be aware that, whether we are with others or alone, we are responsible for our own decisions and actions. Conscience is never absolved by appeal to others. We are to do the right thing, no matter what others, even if their numbers be great, may do.

Perhaps Luke is also thinking of those following Jesus on the way to Calvary as individuals who had hoped that Jesus would liberate them from the tyranny of Rome. But now they realized that this would never be. Jesus had refused to accept the role of political Messiah that they envisioned for Him. As a result, their hopes are dashed to pieces like broken glass.

These disappointed individuals no longer were sympathetic to Jesus. They were angry. Jesus was no different than Judas of Galilee before Him (6 A.D.) or Theudas after Him (46 A.D.). He was just another in the line of false Messiahs that came and went. Both Judas and Theudas had championed a revolt against Rome and led the people to bloodshed. Now, as Jesus faced the fate of all rebels, perhaps those following Jesus in the crowd are there to take revenge, believing that they have been deceived. It is all too easy to place expectations on others and then, when they do not measure up to what we want, to turn against them. It takes real love to accept others for who they are.

Could not some in the crowd along the *Via crucis* have been just casual passers-by? They saw the others following Jesus. They joined with them, if merely to satisfy their curiosity.

A careful reading of the Gospel of Luke shows us who the evangelist sees as the individuals making up the crowd which follows Jesus. Luke places this notice that *"a large crowd of people followed Jesus"* immediately after the conscription of Simon of Cyrene to help Jesus carry His Cross. Simon is forced to carry the Cross. As he is made to follow Jesus as Jesus walks ahead of him, Simon becomes a disciple.

In the Lucan narrative, Simon serves as a positive figure to transition the narrative away from the enemies of Jesus to those who do not oppose Him. For Luke, the crowd is not forced to follow Jesus. These individuals deliberately follow Him along in the crowd. They had come to know something of Jesus during His ministry and there was the beginning of love. Now that He is taken away from them, they are discovering how strong that love is. So often it is separation, and sadly death, that make us realize the value of others in our life.

These good people following Jesus are sympathetic to Him. They may not be disciples. But they are open to discipleship. They are drawn to Jesus in His suffering as they were drawn to Him in His public ministry. There is something that attracts them to Him. It is the attraction to goodness and the inexplicable working of divine grace. It is from this that all discipleship takes its origin.

The Good Thief
Divine Mercy

Three groups of people mock Jesus on the Cross. First, people passing by. They raise their voices and utter blasphemies against Jesus. They mock His claim to destroy the Temple and then rebuild it in three days. They taunt Him to save Himself by coming down from the Cross. But Jesus had taught that *"whoever would save his life will lose it"* (Mk 8:35). These are individuals with no deep knowledge of religion, only great antipathy.

Next the chief priest and scribes jeered at Jesus. Their knowledge of religion is more extensive. But knowledge alone does not save. Even the devils in hell know who Christ is.

This second group is proud. They are unwilling to receive the gift God is offering them in Jesus. They judge themselves already saved. They have set the standard for truth. They are closed to a truth that is greater than any human mind. A Messiah who suffers; a Messiah who is God. They literally "turn their nose at" Jesus for saying He is the Messiah (see Lk 23:35). They challenge Him to come down from the Cross so that they could believe in Him. Theirs is the exact opposite challenge that Jesus gives His disciples: *"Anyone who wishes to follow me must deny himself, take up his cross. . ."* (Mk 8:34).

Lastly, those crucified with Jesus revile Him. Matthew calls them criminals (*"lestai,"* see Mt 27:44). Luke tells us that they are under the same sentence as Jesus Himself (see Lk 23:40-41). These are not the ordinary, run of the mill criminals. These two men on either side of Jesus are rebels. They are freedom fighters who oppose Rome and now are paying the price.

The hostility to Jesus is complete. The casual passer-by, the professional religious, and the criminals: all society is turned against Him. Well could Jesus make His own the words of Psalm 22:7: *"I am reviled by men and considered nothing by the people."*

The criminal to Jesus' left repeats the insults of the others. He has no reason of his own to hate Jesus. But the venom of his own evil heart is found now on his accusing lips. He is the prototype of that individual who does not look into his own soul and face his sin, but instead lashes out at the innocent man and makes Him a victim of his own self-loathing. This criminal does not even tremble before death and judgment before God. He has no faith.

But the criminal to the right confesses his own wrongdoing. He is justly condemned to death. He rebukes the other criminal for his insolence and hardheartedness. *"This man has committed no wrong"* (Lk 23:41), he tells him. Only those who acknowledge their own sins can recognize innocence. Sometimes we hate in others what is wrong in ourselves.

In His suffering, Jesus is broken, but not defeated. He remains loving and even kind to His killers. The criminal witnesses Jesus' prayer of absolution for the world, *"Father, forgive them, for they do not know what they are doing"* (Lk 23:34). True nobility cannot be disguised in suffering. Already on the face of the suffering Christ, the love of heaven shines forth.

Jesus touches this criminal to the right deeply. So moved is he that he makes the most unexpected request of one crucified man to another. With unfeigned sincerity, he pleads: *"Jesus, remember me when you come into your kingdom"* (Lk 23:42). This is the only time in any of the gospels that someone addresses Jesus directly without a title. The moment for formality is past.

"Remember me," the man prays. He asks for mercy. Nothing more. He prays with the humility of the publican who did not dare raise his eyes when he prayed, *"Be merciful to me, a sinner"* (Lk 18:13). His prayer is short. His hope is deep. It is not the length of our prayers that gives them strength, but the intensity of our faith and confidence that make us bold enough to petition.

Jesus is more generous in His response than the criminal could ever have imagined. Jesus now speaks to someone for the very last time in His life. *"Amen, I say to you today you will be with me in Paradise"* (Lk 23:43). Jesus assures him of salvation. He fulfills the mission He inaugurated in the synagogue of Nazareth when He announced His ministry of proclaiming release to captives and setting the oppressed free (see Lk 4:18-19). The criminal will join Jesus in paradise at the banquet with the poor, the lame, and the crippled (see Lk 14:21).

Jesus had said, *"If I be lifted up, I will draw all men to myself"* (Jn 12:32). His prophecy is being fulfilled as the criminal to His right turns to Him in faith. This criminal is literally suffering, dying, and rising with Jesus. His deathbed conversion has turned him into a true disciple—someone who is with Jesus. The Crucified Jesus does not come down from the Cross to save Himself. He remains nailed to its wood to lift us up. His pierced body becomes the overflowing font of mercy to every sinner.

The twelfth century *Gospel of Nicodemus* tells us that the name of the criminal who prays to Jesus on the Cross is Dismas. Another apocryphal gospel relates his earlier years. According to that gospel, Dismas was the leader of a robber band in Egypt. When the Holy Family fled Herod the Great after Jesus' birth, they met up with him. He discerned something special about them and had his men spare them. Thirty years later he saw that child once again, nailed to a Cross (see the sixth century Arabic *Infancy Gospel*). This is simply legend. But the offer of salvation from the Crucified Christ is not!

The scene of the two criminals crucified on either side of Jesus graphically depicts the entire gospel. Jesus is found in the company of sinners. Some accept Him; others do not. The dying man on His right is a sinner, guilty of evil. He has harmed others by his life. He has offended God. Yet, he does not hesitate to turn to Jesus on the Cross and ask for what he does not deserve. Tradition affectionately baptizes this criminal "the good thief." With his dying words, he stole heaven. But, it is good to remember you cannot steal what is being freely given. The good thief is thief no more! His salvation, like ours, is a gift of divine mercy.

John the Beloved
Loyalty

At the very beginning of His public ministry, Jesus chooses John and his brother James as His disciples (see Mk 1:16-20). The two are the sons of Zebedee, a fisherman of some means. The name of their mother is not explicitly stated. However, tradition links Matthew's reference to the mother of Zebedee's children (see Mt 27:56) with Mark's parallel mention of Salome at the Cross (see Mk 15:40) and thereby names Salome, a younger sister of Jesus' own mother, as the mother of James and John. This would make John and his brother cousins of Jesus.

The gospels give John a position of importance among the Twelve Apostles. Beyond his preeminence as one of the first four disciples called by Jesus, he is set apart by the name Jesus gives him. Just as Jesus adds a second name to Simon and calls him Peter, He also gives an epithet to John. Because of their impetuous temper (see Lk 9:54), Jesus calls James and John *"Boanerges."* This Aramaic surname means "sons of thunder" (see Mk 3:17). It is a title that James and

John rightly earn by their quick judgment of others and eager enthusiasm for honor.

John's importance among the followers of Jesus can be inferred from the fact that Jesus singles him out three times for special attention, albeit for a rebuke. When John tells Jesus that the disciples forbade an exorcist who was not one of them from casting out a devil in the name of Jesus (see Mk 9:38-41; Lk 9:49-50), Jesus reprimands him for not understanding Jesus' true mission. When John asked for a special place of honor in the kingdom (see Mk 10:35-45), Jesus again rebukes him. When John and his brother want to call down fire upon the Samaritan village that would not receive Jesus on His journey to Jerusalem, Jesus again reprimands him (see Lk 9:51-56).

Jesus does not pass over lightly the faults of His closest friends. In fact, it is a mark of genuine friendship to correct a friend (see Prov 27:5-6). John clearly enjoys an intimate friendship with Jesus. He is one of the three disciples Jesus takes with Him when He raises Jairus' daughter from the dead, when He is transfigured in glory on the mountain, and when He privately gives His teaching on the end time. Jesus trusts John.

He allows him to see what others would not understand. Only in the context of authentic friendship is self-revelation possible.

From the very beginning of his call, John is found always in the company of Peter: at the cure of Peter's mother-in-law (see Mk 1:29-31), in the home of Jairus (see Mk 5:37), on the Mount of Transfiguration (see Mk 9:2), on the Mount of Olives (see Mk 13:3), in the preparations for the Last Supper (see Lk 22:8), in the Garden of Gethsemane (see Mk 14:33), and at the house of the high priest (see Jn 18:15). But there is one time Peter and John part company. During the Passion, both follow Jesus along the road to Calvary. But only John takes the journey to the foot of the Cross.

Some had followed Jesus with the hope of a political Messiah who would bring them security and freedom from Rome. They were looking for more bread, more wine, more good things of this world. Unlike these "friends," with Jesus when there is something to be gained, John remains with Jesus when every hope of worldly success has been stripped away (see Prov 14:20; 19:4). True friendship is unconditional (see Prov 17:17).

As Ruth remained bound to her mother-in-law Naomi in times of trouble, as David continued to love his closest friend Jonathan slain in battle, John loves Jesus to the end. John brings to life the words of Proverbs 18:24: *"a friend is more loyal than a brother."*

False friendship ruins the human heart. But a friendship that is loyal and true reveals the very heart of the God who says to us who are so unfaithful *"Ephraim, how could I part with you: Israel, how could I give you up?"* (Hos 11:8). Faithfulness and loyalty are love in deed. John at the foot of the Cross is the loyal friend. Like John, we remain loyal to Jesus when we do not stop trusting in Him, loving Him, even in the midst of sufferings too great to understand.

STATIONS
of the
CROSS

1. Jesus Is Condemned to Death

O Jesus, help me to appreciate Your sanctifying grace more and more.

2. Jesus Bears His Cross

O Jesus, You chose to die for me. Help me to love You always with all my heart.

3. Jesus Falls the First Time

O Jesus, make me strong to conquer my wicked passions, and to rise quickly from sin.

4. Jesus Meets His Mother

O Jesus, grant me a tender love for Your Mother, who offered You for love of me.

5. Jesus Is Helped by Simon

O Jesus, like Simon lead me ever closer to You through my daily crosses and trials.

6. Jesus and Veronica

O Jesus, imprint Your image on my heart that I may be faithful to You all my life.

7. Jesus Falls a Second Time

O Jesus, I repent for having offended You. Grant me forgiveness of all my sins.

8. Jesus Speaks to the Women

O Jesus, grant me tears of compassion for Your sufferings and of sorrow for my sins.

STATICS
of the
CROSS

9. Jesus Falls a Third Time

O Jesus, let me never yield to despair. Let me come to You in hardship and spiritual distress.

10. He Is Stripped of His Garments

O Jesus, let me sacrifice all my attachments rather than imperil the divine life of my soul.

11. Jesus Is Nailed to the Cross

O Jesus, strengthen my faith and increase my love for You. Help me to accept my crosses.

12. Jesus Dies on the Cross

O Jesus, I thank You for making me a child of God. Help me to forgive others.

STATIONS
of the
CROSS

13. Jesus Is Taken Down from the Cross

O Jesus, through the intercession of Your holy Mother, let me be pleasing to You.

14. Jesus Is Laid in the Tomb

O Jesus, strengthen my will to live for You on earth and bring me to eternal bliss in heaven.

Prayer after the Stations

JESUS, You became an example of humility, obedience and patience, and preceded me on the way of life bearing Your Cross. Grant that, inflamed with Your love, I may cheerfully take upon myself the sweet yoke of Your Gospel together with the mortification of the Cross and follow You as a true disciple so that I may be united with You in heaven. Amen.

10 Mary
The Birth of the Church

All the gospels mention that there are women at the crucifixion: Mary Magdalene, Mary the mother of James and Joseph, and Salome, the mother of James and John (see Mt 27:55-56; Mk 15:40; Lk 23:49). These women had followed Jesus in His public ministry and had assisted Him from their own means. The men flee. But the women remain with Jesus to the end. Love is the soul of fidelity. Loyalty endures the test of suffering. No one loved Him more than His own mother. She accompanied Him in His public ministry (see Mk 3:35). She is with Him until the end. As the fourth evangelist tells us, *"There stood by the Cross of Jesus His mother"* (Jn 19:25).

In John's gospel Mary is present at the wedding feast of Cana. But, afterwards, she is conspicuously absent from the scene. She is never mentioned at all—until the Cross. John alone tells us that the mother of Jesus is present on Calvary. The mother is drawn to the Son in the hour of His suffering.

The danger Jesus faced in His public ministry was well known. When Jesus is on His way to Judea to raise Lazarus from the dead, the disciples try to keep Him from going. They know that the plot is already forming to do away with Him. But when Jesus refuses to heed their warning, Thomas says, *"Let us also go that we may die with him"* (Jn 11:16).

Mary knows the danger as well as anyone else. That is why she chooses to be in Jerusalem, near her son. The mother clings to her children like ivy to the castle wall. Neither the summer sun nor the winter cold can tear them apart. A mother's love brings Mary to the foot of the Cross.

Mary is no stranger to sorrow. When she is about to give birth, she endures the hardship of travel from Nazareth to Bethlehem so that her son could be born in the City of David. When Herod is looking to kill her infant son, she and Joseph flee into Egypt. When the religious leaders turn against her son, she suffers. When the people reject Him, her heart is heavy with grief.

When Jesus was presented as a child in the Temple, the old man Simeon prophesied this suffering. He told Mary: *"A sword shall pierce through your own heart"* (Lk 2:35). The soldier's lance will soon run through the heart of Christ at His death. But already, as Jesus is dying, the sword of sorrow pierces the maternal heart of Mary.

Mary was the first to place a kiss on His brow. She had quenched His thirst and caressed Him with tenderness. Now His hands are nailed to a tree; His brow bleeding; His throat parched. A mother never abandons her child. His pain is her suffering. His death, her broken heart. Never had the world seen a mother's heart filled with such joy at the birth of a child. Never will it see such sorrow at His death. Who could ever fathom the depth of a mother's love!

Matthew, Mark, and Luke all place the other women on Golgotha "at a distance" from the Cross. But John places Mary right next to the cross. The woman closest to Jesus in life is closest to Him in death. Love gives Mary the courage to be there. There is no love in nature stronger than the bond of mother and child.

The crowd is drunk with mockery. The criminal to the left is hurling insults. The one to the right, begging for mercy. Mary is silent. With loud cries and lamentation,

Rachel weeps at the death of her children (see Jer 31:15). But not one word from Mary's lips. There are sorrows that cannot be spoken. The deepest sorrow sheds silent tears.

As Jesus was always faithful to the Father, Mary was always faithful to the Son. Her presence at the foot of the Cross is the gift of her total union with her son in the work of redemption. Mary stands. It is the position of nobility. She causes her son no added pain by loud laments. At the death of her son's cruel execution, Rizpah throws herself on the ground in uncontrollable grief (see 2 Sam 23:10-11). Mary stands. It is the proper gesture for one who is sacrificing. The Shepherd is willingly laying down His life as the Lamb led to slaughter. Jesus is the Victim. Mary is one with Him in self-immolation.

With thorn-crowned head, Jesus looks down from the Cross. He speaks. He reveals Mary's new role in God's plan of salvation. *"Seeing his mother and the disciple whom he loved standing near her, Jesus said to his mother, 'Woman, behold your son.' Then to the disciple he said, 'Behold your mother'"* (Jn 19:26-27).

The fourth evangelist does not place the personal names of either Mary or John on the lips of the crucified Jesus. The evangelist knows their names as well as he knows his own. But he never uses them in his gospel. Rather, he uses their titles. He wants us to see these individuals in their roles for the entire Church, not in their personal relations.

Jesus spoke and water turned to wine. His word multiplied bread and called Lazarus from the grave. Christ's word has power. It effects what it commands. He speaks now from the Cross. And His word creates a new reality, a new relationship in the economy of salvation.

"Son, behold your mother." Jesus first entrusts the beloved disciple to Mary. Mary is to care for the disciple. Clearly, Jesus is not simply making provisions for the earthly care of His mother after His death. To the beloved, Jesus gifts His own mother. He is not renouncing the bond that binds Him to Mary. He is elevating and expanding it. The beloved disciple is every true believer. Mary's motherhood is universal. We are all placed in her care.

"Woman, behold your son." It is the second Annunciation. At the word of the angel, Mary became the mother of the Son of God.

At the word of the Son of God, she now becomes the mother of all God's children.

The Cross is the "hour" of redemption. It is the moment when God's plan for our salvation is accomplished. According to that plan, every disciple is now bound to Mary in the order of grace. She is our mother, not just for a time, but for all eternity. In the birth pangs of Golgotha, the Church is born. And, at the center, there beats the heart of a mother.

The Centurion
Faith

As Mark recounts the details of the Crucifixion, he draws heavily from the Old Testament. Jesus is crucified between two criminals (see Isa 53:12). Those who see Him deride and mock him (see Ps 22:7-8; Ps 69:8; Lam 2:15). The soldiers divide His garments by casting lots (see Ps 22:19). They offer Him wine to drink (see Ps 69:22; Prov 31:6-7). Jesus voices His utter sense of abandonment with the opening line of Psalm 22.

These Old Testament allusions all speak of the righteous man who suffers. They serve to interpret the historical event of the Crucifixion. Jesus is the Just One, the Innocent One, who suffers and is vindicated in His death. The Cross is part of God's plan. Mark will end his account of the Crucifixion with the centurion's confession of this truth.

The centurion who stands on Calvary sees in the dying Christ something he never saw before. The Romans regularly crucified the enemies of the state: rebels, murderers, revolutionaries, and captives taken in war.

75

So cruel was this form of execution that the Romans would never crucify one of their own citizens. Those who were crucified would die a most painful death. Their cries and blasphemies would fill the air. They would curse both God and man. But the centurion hears no curse from Jesus' lips. He sees beyond the Victim nailed to the Cross.

Those crucified with Jesus hurl their abusive speech at Him. Those passing by throw His own words in His face as an insult: *"You who would destroy the temple and rebuild it in three days, save yourself, if you are the Son of God, [and] come down from the cross!"* (Mt 27:40). The leaders of the people take His many deeds of compassion, healing the sick, giving sight to the blind, and raising the dead to life, and fling them at Him in derision: *"He saved others; he cannot save himself. . . . Let him come down from the cross now, and we will believe in him"* (Mt 27:42).

They are right. Jesus has power over His own life. He himself said, *"No one takes it from me, but I lay it down on my own. I have power to lay it down, and power to take it up again"* (Jn 10:8). But, they are mistaken in their demand for Him to come down from the Cross. *"The Son of Man did not come to be served but to serve and to give his life as a ransom for many"* (Mt 20:28). He stays on the Cross. He does not come down. No, He takes us up with Him to the Father.

Roman law is visiting injustice on Jesus. His own people are rejecting Him. His friends have abandoned Him. His enemies are reviling Him. Yet, Jesus remains the master of His own life. There are no words of resentment against an abusive author-ity. No coarse curses for His enemies. No wounded reproof of His friends. No hatred. No vengeance. No evil.

On two occasions when Jesus had cast out Satan from the possessed, the devil came out defeated, shrieking with a loud cry (*phone megale*: see Mk 1:26; 5:7). Now, on the Cross, Jesus exemplifies His own teaching *"to love your enemies, do good to those who hate you, bless those who curse you, pray for those who mistreat you"* (Lk 6:27-28), Jesus loves us to His dying breath. Jesus has faced the ugly reality of Satan's power in this world. All the evil that ever oppressed God's children from the time of Adam is pressing in on Jesus. Yet, He remains unshaken in His love. As He dies, He shouts out with a loud cry *"phone megale"* (Mk 15:34-37). Satan has been cast out.

The centurion at the Cross had seen many men of valor die heroically on the battlefield. But the heroism of Jesus surpasses their stoic endurance. His calm, His self-mastery, His unexpected words of forgiveness are unparalleled. They reveal a depth of moral greatness never seen before. No guilty man could ever die like this.

The biblical allusions from Psalm 69 and Psalm 22 woven throughout the Passion story find voice in the words of the centurion. Moved by the goodness of Jesus, the centurion exclaims, *"This man was just beyond doubt"* (Lk 23:47). Rome had unjustly condemned Jesus. Now Rome exonerates Him. Paradoxically, the innocent Jesus dying for the guilty overturns the verdict of guilt that our sins justly deserve.

In the earliest preaching of the Church, Jesus is called "the Just One." Peter uses this title in preaching the gospel after the cure of the lame man in the temple (see Acts 3:14). Stephen uses it in his speech before being martyred (see Acts 7:52). Ananias tells Paul that God had chosen him to see the Just One (see Acts 22:14). By calling

Jesus "just" at the moment of His death, the centurion has on his lips the very preaching of the Church.

As in Matthew's gospel, so also in Mark's, the centurion recognizes Jesus' deepest identity. He cries out, *"Truly this man was the Son of God!"* (Mk 15:39.). In this confession of faith is the confession of the Church who proclaims in the Nicene Creed that Jesus is *"the Only Begotten Son of the Father. . . God from God, true light from true light, true God from true God, begotten, not made, consubstantial with the Father."* Jesus is no mere man. He is God made man. This is the faith that moves believers in every age to give their lives to Jesus.

Joseph *"went in to Pilate and asked for the body of Jesus"* (Mt 27:58). His burial of Jesus is his act of love for the Lord.

12 Joseph of Arimathea
The Work of Charity

The Jews believed that worse than being put to death as a criminal was leaving the dead person's corpse exposed to shame and humiliation. This brought the executed the added public disgrace of having his flesh devoured by wild birds. The punishment of being hanged on a tree and left to the elements was thought to be so severe, that it was reserved only for "this one accursed of God" (see Deut 21:23). Paul expounds on this when he says: *"Christ has redeemed us from the curse of the law, having become a curse for us, for it is written, 'Cursed is everyone who hangs on a tree' "* (Gal 3:13-14).

Jewish law tempered its justice with mercy. The humiliation to the memory of the executed criminal and his family must not be excessive. The law demanded that *"If a man guilty of a capital offense is put to death and his corpse hung on a tree, it shall not remain on the tree overnight. You shall bury it the same day"* (Deut 21:22-23). This law, this mercy, is what prompts Joseph of Arimathea to go to Pilate and ask for the body of Jesus. He wants to bury Jesus before sunset on Good Friday.

Joseph's membership in the Jewish highest court would certainly explain why he had easy access to Pilate with his request to bury the body of Jesus and why Pilate so readily granted his wish. The procurator was not a man to receive just anyone without prior notice. Yet, Joseph *"went in to Pilate and asked for the body of Jesus"* (Mt 27:58).

Pilate would not have been eager to give the body of Jesus to a known disciple of Jesus. He feared that the disciples were going to stage a resurrection. But, he would have had no problem handing over Jesus' body to one who belonged to the very court that had condemned Jesus to death. No fear that the Jews would make Jesus into a martyr figure.

Joseph is a good and righteous man who respects the law. Both Mark and Luke tell us that Joseph was *"awaiting the kingdom of God"* (Mk 15:43; see Lk 23:51). The disciples of Jesus were not the only ones expecting the arrival of the Kingdom of God. They believed that Jesus Himself would be the one to free them from the tyranny of Rome and usher in God's kingdom in their day. But there were many other devout Jews who did not believe in Jesus. Yet, they were still waiting for the Kingdom of God. These Jews would scrupulously observe all the commandments in order to prepare for the coming of God's kingdom. Joseph most assuredly belonged to this group.

However, Matthew identifies Joseph of Arimathea as a disciple (see Mt 27:57). And, John says that he was *"a disciple of Jesus, though a secret one because he was afraid of the Jews"* (Jn 19:38). Already during the trial of Jesus, Joseph had showed his sympathy for Him. All the other members accused Jesus of blasphemy and condemned Him to death. But Joseph *"did not consent to their purpose and deed"* (Lk 23:51).

During the unjust process that brought Jesus to the Cross, Joseph stood out. He followed his conscience and did not give in to the pressure of the group. He refused to cast his vote with the majority when they were clearly in the wrong. People of good conscience are often placed in this position. Too often leaders set in place policies, laws, and programs that violate moral standards with the excuse that this is what the majority wants. They fear standing apart. They fear losing their status. When principle is at stake and the life of an innocent person at any stage is on the line, a right conscience must never yield to party loyalty or personal security.

What a model Joseph of Arimathea is for those in government or in the private sector to hold on to principle over pragmatism, individual responsibility over camaraderie. One individual who takes a courageous stand for what is good will always embolden others to follow. It is no surprise, then, that when Joseph of Arimathea comes to bury Jesus, he is joined by Nicodemus.

It was more than a simple act of piety that prompts Joseph to bury Jesus' body. In witnessing the sufferings of Jesus, he comes to love the Lord even more. No more fear. *"Love casts out fear"* (1 Jn 4:18). His burial of Jesus is his act of love for the Lord. Such love secures Joseph of Arimathea a place in all four gospels as well as later apocryphal works that list him as a true disciple.

Faith in the Lord always leads to works of charity. *"As the body without the spirit is dead, so faith without works is also dead"* (Jas 2:26). The greater our faith in Jesus, the greater our efforts to do good to others.

Mary Magdalene
The Empty Tomb

Mary Magdalene first appears in the last gospel at the Cross. The first three gospel writers show us Mary standing in the distance. However, the fourth gospel moves Mary to the foot of the Cross (see Jn 19:25). The direction is theological. Lifted up, Jesus is already drawing His scattered disciples into the new family born in the blood of the Cross. Although John never mentions Mary Magdalene as following Jesus before this moment, he now shows her as refusing to leave Him.

All the gospels report Mary's visit to the tomb. Memories crowd their accounts. Details differ as their pen rushes to report the Resurrection. It is John who tells us the most of Mary's Sunday morning visit. Though he writes after Mark, Matthew, and Luke, he passes on to us the best historical tradition of the event.

Each evangelist notes that when Joseph and Nicodemus bury the body of Jesus, there are women present (see Mt 27:61; Mk 15:47; Lk 23:55-56). Mary Magdalene and

Mary the mother of Joses are there. They watch, but they do not take part in the burial. Jesus is dead. Her hope extinguished. Yet love remains. The male disciples have disappeared. No future; no presence. Yet Mary lingers.

Mark tells us that Mary Magdalene kept observing (see Mk 15:47: *etheōroun*, the imperfect of the Greek verb). She could not remove her eyes any more than she could withdraw her love from Jesus. Joseph of Arimathea and Nicodemus entomb Jesus. Mary is already planning to return to anoint the body with spices once the Sabbath is ended. Evening begins to fall. The darkness thickens within. She returns home for the night.

Early on the first day of the week, she returns. Love never rests. It is still dark, but the Light is already scattering the darkness. Rabbinic tradition held that mourning for the dead was at its greatest on the third day. Mary's grief is intense. Like those bereaved of a loved one, she visits the cemetery. Closeness to the grave somehow eases the separation. Through her tears, she sees the stone has been rolled away. The body is gone. Disappointment hastens her steps to tell the others.

Peter and the Beloved Disciple run to the tomb. Mary has told the truth. The tomb is empty. No time to waste at a hollow grave. They return home. But Mary Magdalene remains. Her tears cannot wash away the horror. The body has been stolen. Love's final farewell denied.

Magdalene peers into the gaping hole carved into the side of the hill. Where the body had been, two angels sit, one at the head and the other at the foot. Angels hovered over the cradle where love was born. Angels keep guard over the sepulcher where love triumphs over death. Mary still weeps. No angel can fill the emptiness of her heart. The empty tomb did not give rise to Easter faith. Even in its stillness, it spoke of death. Only the appearances of the Risen Lord moved the disciples from despair to faith.

As Mary turns from the tomb, Mary sees the Risen Lord. At first, she does not recognize Him. In all the appearances of the Risen Lord, Jesus is not immediately known. The two disciples on the road to Emmaus do not recognize Jesus even as they walk and talk with Him. They only come to know Him when they sit at table for the breaking of the bread (see Lk 24:13-35). The disciples who

returned to the Sea of Tiberias to take up
their former profession as fishermen see the
Lord. They talk to Him about fishing. Only
after the Beloved Disciple says, *"It is the
Lord,"* do they recognize Jesus (Jn 21:1-8).

Jesus has been raised from the dead. It
is Resurrection, not resuscitation. He has
not returned to his former earthly life. He
has been raised up to the glory of God. The
body is His, but He is transformed. The
appearances of the Risen Lord have stopped
long ago. But, we who believe today are in
no way at a disadvantage. Mere sight of the
Risen Lord does not produce Easter faith.
Only a heart willing to enter a new relationship with Jesus as Lord knows Easter faith.

At first, Mary thinks Jesus is the garden-
er. Sorrow clouds her vision. She accuses
Him of taking away the body. Jesus says but
one word, *"Mary."* Her name. The tenderness unmistakable. *"Rabbouni, Teacher,"*
her quick response. *"The sheep hear his
voice; one by one he calls them by name"* (Jn
10:3). The Good Shepherd is gathering His
scattered sheep (see Jn 10:14-16).

It is the word that Jesus speaks to Mary
and her welcoming that word that gifts her
with Easter faith. It is the same word that

Jesus continues to speak in His Church to us. By accepting the word proclaimed in the *praeconium paschale* and in the preaching of the Church, we enter into our dialogue of faith with the Risen Lord.

Joy overwhelms Mary's heart. As Matthew tells us, she falls down and grasps Jesus (see Mt 28:9). Love desires permanence. *"Do not keep clinging to me,"* Jesus tells Mary (Jn 20:17). Jesus will remain. He will not leave us orphans (see Jn 14:18). Through the mystery of His death and resurrection, He ascends to the Father. Because He goes to the Father, He now sends the Spirit (see Jn 16:7-8). Through the Spirit, Jesus remains with His disciples and so does the Father (see Jn 14:23-26). We become the very dwelling place of the Trinity. What an Easter gift! The tomb is empty; our hearts are full. Like Mary, our souls are flooded with joy of the God's Presence that no one can take from us.

Love enkindles love. And so Jesus sends Mary to bring the good news of the Resurrection to the others. To women as well as to men, the Lord entrusts divine truths. In His commission given to Mary, the Risen Lord fulfills the words of the Prophet:

"I will pour out my spirit on all flesh; your sons and your daughters shall prophesy" (Joel 3:1; see *Mulieris Dignitatem*, 16).

Through the word of Jesus, Mary Magdalene came to faith. Now she bears that word to others. First in the gospels to see the Risen Lord, first to share the good news with others. Mary Magdalene is as tradition rightly calls her, *"the apostle to the apostles"* (Rabanus Maurus, *De vita beatae Mariae Magdalenae*, XXVII). Those who truly believe always become, like Mary, eager to tell others of the joy of knowing the Risen Lord.

Conclusion

As angels had hovered over Jesus' cradle, they likewise attended His tomb. In the still of the night, they filled the skies of Bethlehem with the first *Gloria in excelsis Deo*, heralding the good news of Jesus' birth. In the hushed silence of the garden tomb, they filled the hearts of three grieving women with joy brighter than the rising sun.

To Mary Magdalene, Mary, the mother of James, and Salome the wife of Zebedee, an angel announced that Jesus had risen from the dead. The tomb was empty. The Cross is a victory. Death and sin are not the last words.

Startled and half-believing, the women hurried to tell the apostles. Jesus had been raised up. He is no longer among the dead. This is the single most important fact of all history. Jesus is Lord. As Risen Lord who once called Peter to follow Him even to the Cross, He calls each of us.

The Easter message gives us strength to respond to His call. By Hs Resurrection, He gifts us with the Holy Spirit who enables us to face life's bitter disappointments and even death itself. The widow standing at a fresh grave; the mother cradling her lifeless child, the handicapped, the victim of violence, war, and poverty, the lonely and the abandoned, the sick, the terminally ill, those burdened with sorrow: each of us, filled with His Spirit, stands in wonder before the empty tomb. God has the last word. And it is life!

We look into the empty tomb and see the bright promise of our own bodily resurrection. We have already died with Christ in baptism and have risen with Him to new life in the Spirit (see Rm 6:4-6). And, one day—and it is sure to come—the Father will raise us up bodily from our dusty graves to heaven's glory. For those united to Christ Crucified and Risen, God will take every sorrow and turn it into sweetness. He will transform all grief into glory. And, even now, He makes the sunset of death itself give way to the dawning of eternal life.

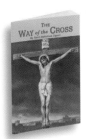

THE WAY OF THE CROSS — By St. Alphonsus Liguori. This booklet is a devotion to the Sacred Passion of our Lord. We follow Him from when He was condemned to death to His being laid in the tomb. 32 pages. Size 3⅞ x 6¼.

No. 14/05—Flexible cover .... **.95**
ISBN 978-0-89942-014-1
Also Available in Spanish: El Camino de la Cruz
No. 16/S ISBN 978-0-89942-016-5 .... **.95**

THROUGH HIS WOUNDS WE ARE HEALED — By Vojtĕch Kodet, O. Carm. This brief but profound book helps us to more fully understand how the Way of the Cross can be a wonderful means of uniting ourselves and the difficulties in our lives more intimately with Christ and His sufferings. 64 pages. Size 4 x 6¼.

No. 116/04—Flexible cover **3.95**
ISBN 978-0-89942-116-2

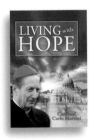

LIVING WITH HOPE — By Cardinal Carlo Maria Martini, S.J. Reflecting on the author's pastoral thoughts on the actions and teachings of Jesus and the Church will help us to live in Christian hope and proclaim this hope to others. 192 pages. Size 5¼ x 7¾.

No. 167/04—Flexible cover **8.95**
ISBN 978-1-937913-78-6

DAILY MEDITATIONS WITH THE HOLY SPIRIT — By Rev. Jude Winkler, OFM Conv. Through daily Scripture readings and prayer, Fr. Winkler offers us an opportunity to develop a closer relationship with the Holy Spirit and to apply the fruits of our meditation to our everyday lives. 192 pages. Size 4 x 6¼.

No. 198/19—Dura-Lux cover **8.95**
ISBN 978-1-937913-56-4

FOLLOWING THE HOLY SPIRIT — A valuable book for all who want to learn more about the Holy Spirit and His vital role in the lives of all Catholics. Large type, pleasing format, and beautiful illustrations. 288 pages. Size 4 x 6¼.

No. 335/19—Dura-Lux cover **8.95**
ISBN 978-0-89942-340-1

MARY DAY BY DAY — Minute Marian meditations for every day of the year, including a Scripture passage, a quotation from the Saints, and a concluding prayer. Printed in two colors with over 300 illustrations. 192 pages. Size 4 x 6¼.

No. 180/19—Dura-Lux cover **8.95**
ISBN 978-1-937913-07-6

UPLIFTING THOUGHTS FOR EVERY DAY — By Rev. John Catoir. We can eliminate negative thinking and improve our emotional life by filling our mind with uplifting thoughts. 192 pages. Size 4 x 6¼.

No. 197/19—Dura-Lux cover **8.95**
ISBN 978-1-937913-02-1

THE JOY OF LENT — By Pat McDonough. Reflections of Catholic statesmen, theologians, bishops, and parents to inspire readers to re-think the traditional practices of fasting, prayer, and almsgiving. 96 pages. Size 5 x 7.

No. RP 172/04—Flexible cover... **2.95**
ISBN 978-1-878718-77-8

MY POCKET WAY OF THE CROSS — by St. Alphonsus Liguori. With glorious full-color illustrations, this pocket- or purse-size book offers those who wish to pray the Stations a handy companion for this popular devotion on the Sacred Passion of Our Lord. 48 pages. Size 2¹/₂ x 3³/₄.

No. 18/04—Flexible cover..............**1.25**
ISBN 978-1-937913-30-4

THE LITANY OF THE SACRED HEART — By Mario Collantes. This collection of 33 invocations with accompanying commentaries offers a meaningful way to express and nurture our love for the Person of Jesus, Who is the Source of our salvation and hope. Full color. 96 pages. Size 4³/₈ x 6³/₄.

No. 374/04—Flexible cover............ **5.95**
ISBN 978-0-89942-366-1

JOYFULLY LIVING THE GOSPEL DAY BY DAY — By Rev. John Catoir. Each day contains a specific Scripture quotation, reflection, and prayer to encourage joyous participation in the Christian life. 192 pages. Size 4 x 6¹/₄.

No. 188/19—Dura-Lux cover **8.95**
ISBN 978-1-937913-04-5

THE IMITATION OF CHRIST — by Thomas à Kempis. Prayer book size edition. This treasured book has brought peace to readers for many ages by showing how to follow the life of Christ to which all are called. Includes a full-color Rosary and Stations of the Cross section. 288 pages. Size 4 x 6¹/₄.

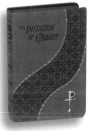

No. 320/19—Dura-Lux cover **9.95**
ISBN 978-1-941243-16-9

St. Joseph CATHOLIC MANUAL — By Rev. Thomas J. Donaghy. A digest of the most important Catholic beliefs, the most popular Catholic prayers, and the most prominent Catholic practices. It is completely indexed to the Catechism of the Catholic Church. Printed in two colors. 96 pages. Size $5^3/_8$ x $7^1/_4$.

No. 268/04—Flexible cover....**3.75**
ISBN 978-0-89942-268-8

St. Joseph GUIDE TO THE BIBLE — By Karl A. Schultz. This small volume will help readers select a Bible, develop a reading plan, practice *lectio divina*, and begin to interpret the Bible with competence and confidence. 144 pages. Size 5 x 7.

No. 656/04—Flexible cover...... **7.95**
ISBN 978-0-89942-657-0

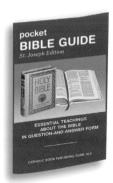

POCKET BIBLE GUIDE — St. Joseph Edition — Handy, pocket-sized booklet that will help Catholics know what the Bible is and prepare them to read it with understanding. The "Questions and Answers" section provides essential teachings of the Church about the Bible. Illustrated in full color. 64 pages. Size 4 x $6^1/_2$.

No. 56/00—Flexible cover.........**1.95**
ISBN 978-0-89942-056-1